W9-BIB-400

MEDITATIONS ON JOY

MEDITATIONS ON
JOY

BY JANET ELA LEBOUTILLIER

WINGS BOOKS ■ NEW YORK ■ NEW JERSEY

Random House
New York • Toronto • London • Sydney • Auckland

Jacket art: Paradise, Maurice Denis
Design: Nora Sheehan
Production supervision by Roméo Enriquez

Printed and bound in Mexico

Library of Congress Cataloging-in-Publication Data

LeBoutillier, Janet, Ela.
Meditations on Joy / Janet Ela LeBoutillier.
p.   cm.
ISBN 0-517-12414-9
1. Joy—Religious aspects—Meditations.   2. Self-actualization (Psychology)—
Religious aspects—Meditations.   I. Title.
BL626.35.L43   1995   95-14505
158'.12—dc20   CIP

8   7   6   5   4   3   2   1

ABOUT THE AUTHOR

Janet Ela LeBoutillier is a mother, daughter, grandmother, wife, retired real estate investment executive, and writer. She has been involved in meditation, contemplation, healing prayer, and prayer ministry as a seeker, a vessel, and a servant.

TODAY

Today, whatever may annoy,
The word for me is Joy, just simple joy:
The joy of life;
The joy of children and of wife;
The joy of bright, blue skies;
The joy of rain; the glad surprise
Of twinkling stars that shine at night;
The joy of winged things upon their flight;
The joy of noonday, and the tried
The joyousness of eventide;
The joy of labor, and of mirth;
The joy of air, and sea, and earth—
The countless joys that ever flow from Him
Whose vast beneficence doth dim
The lustrous light of day,
And lavish gifts divine upon our way.
Whate'er there be of Sorrow
I'll put off til Tomorrow,
And when Tomorrow comes, why then
'Twill be Today and Joy again!

JOHN KENDRICK BANGS

WATERLILIES AT SUNSET, CLAUDE MONET

There is that in me—I do not know what it is—/but I know it is in me. . . .
To it the creation is the friend whose embracing/awakes me. . . .
It is not chaos or death—it is form, union, plan—/it is eternal life—it is Happiness.
WALT WHITMAN

Happiness and joy mean embracing, loving, and harmonizing with divine creation. The kingdom within and the kingdom without fuse. How do we access that part of ourselves so that we are awakened to our spiritual nature? Take the grating, blaring noise and lurching, whizzing weave of a subway or major highway. The seeming chaos influences our thinking, emotions, and behavior. Anxiety, anger, aggression, scowling, disgust, withdrawal, and so on emerge. But we have choices. Will you allow yourself to be influenced in this negative way or will you decide to change and seek happiness? First choose to become still. Let your higher nature observe your thoughts and feelings of anxiety, worries about the future, things to do. Visualize light surrounding these negative creations of your mind, and let the wind of spirit carry them from you. Awesome, isn't it, how the whizzing weave has become an orderly flow of people, machines, and technology; the grating noise is now an integrated song of the wheels of transportation. Perception of people, places, and things is altered. Choosing to let go of the big *I* and choosing union with this power outside of ourselves enables us to see, hear, and feel the world around us from the view point of spirit. In these moments spirit illuminates eternal love. Joy and happiness blossom as we see the world anew.

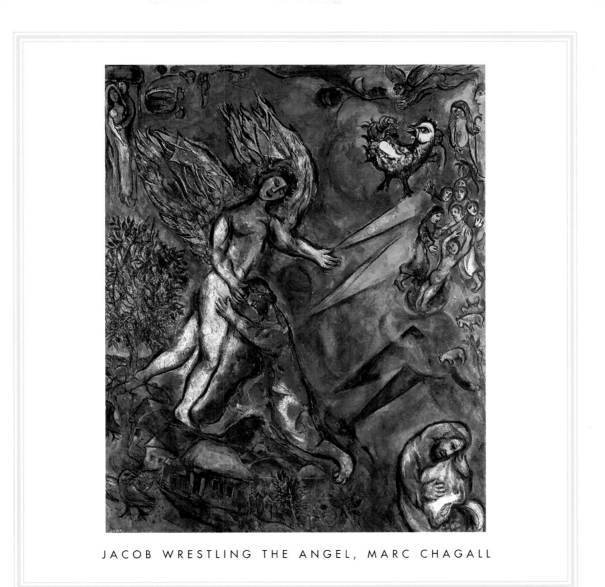

JACOB WRESTLING THE ANGEL, MARC CHAGALL

Love is; quarrels are made. Joy is; unhappiness is made.
Truth is; falsehoods are made. Life is; sickness is made.

DR. GLENN CLARK

Life embodies the spirit of love, joy, and truth. It was. It is. It will be. Opposites are made when we are not in unity with the eternal truths of the Creator. How often the little things can disrupt the rhythm of love, such as the happy breakfast that is suddenly disrupted by a cup of spilled milk. The mother yells, the boy cries and unhappiness replaces joy as love and unity are violated. This doesn't have to happen. Clean away the mess cheerfully. There is no need to make it more than it is. And in the process you are teaching your child the loving way to mop up a little mess. Don't we all spill something sometimes? We are all responsible to some degree for quarrels, unhappiness, errors, and negative feelings affecting our wellness. Ignorance and willfulness limit us and the world we live in. What is your relationship with God? What do you know about the unseen vital spirit at work in your life and the world around you? Our words and actions reflect our relationship with and obedience to this infinite source. Be spiritually attuned and no longer will you drift into devil-made harbors of discomfort. You will glide over the waves and winds of the subtle, changing rhythms of life in love, truth, and joy. Wake up to the truth. Desire and expect to know intimately the divine spirit speaking through your soul. Begin to realize it now.

MATERNITY WITH A RED CURTAIN, PABLO PICASSO

It is only in sorrow bad weather masters us;
in joy we face the storm and defy it.

AMELIA BARR

Joy strengthens us. Joy lightens ordeals in our lives. When we get stuck in the sorrow of distressing times and places, new problems become even more difficult. The weight of burdens holds us down; we are no longer living. ■ When you encounter these poor souls, do you ever ask yourself what makes the difference? Take for example two young men raised in the same dysfunctional family. Their father died of alcoholism; their mother remarried and continued her life as a pleasure seeker. They were sent away to boarding school at a young age. The older brother lived a constructive adventurous life. The other brother existed in desperation, indulging in destructive behaviors. ■ Both young men were asked, "Tell me about your life as a young boy. What was important? What was difficult?" The sad, corpse-like brother said, "Everything was wrong. My father died and left me. My step-father took my mother away from me. In boarding school I couldn't do what I wanted. I have to work because my mother won't give me money." The other brother responded, "It was hard when my father died. But boarding school opened up a whole new world to me. It was really better than being home. Beyond the three Rs, I learned values, discipline, sports; it was one big family of brothers." Same circumstances, same events. What was different? ■ Yesterday's sorrows mastered the one brother. The self-pitying "me" was drowning the Thou. He stopped living. The past tragedy of the other brother was seen as an opportunity, a new chance. Living became an adventure. Life unfolding yielded joy and strengthened him for all new hurdles. Around each turn, through the valleys and over every mountain, joy and life awaited him. And he knew it.

RAINBOW OVER THE GRAND CANYON OF
THE YELLOWSTONE, THOMAS MORAN

It is good to tame the mind, which is often difficult to hold in and flighty, rushing wherever it listeth; a disciplined mind brings happiness.

BUDDHIST SCRIPTURES

Watch your thoughts. Where does your mental meandering take you? Into the shadows of doubt and fear? To the pinnacle of fruitless fantasy? Has a song ever taken you on a roller-coaster mind trip through painful nostalgia? Have you tried training your mind? ■ All too often our minds run amuck. For example, the husband whose professional wife takes occasional business trips with male associates may misinterpret a friendly business conversation. The escalating thoughts lead to anger and anxiety over a divorce because of an imaginary affair. Are circumstances robbing you of joy? ■ Guard your mind with the armor of light. Protect it from the destructive thoughts and emotions that attack the gates and take command. A Latin proverb, "When the pilot does not know what port he is heading for, no wind is the right wind" describes the confused person buffeted by a lack of mental control. The mind is the rudder; the body, the boat; the wind and water, life's circumstances; the compass or stars, the guiding light. ■ Cultivate the single mind. Bring your attention back to the light in the eye of life's storms and be led back to your highest purpose. Do this as often as you are aware of being off course. As the mind learns discipline and its higher purpose, distractions cease to steal the moment. Joy is enjoyed. ■ A disciplined mind contemplates God—His pure, brilliant light—and the mind is illuminated from within. According to Buddha, "What you think you become." Serve the light. Let it in and brighten the world.

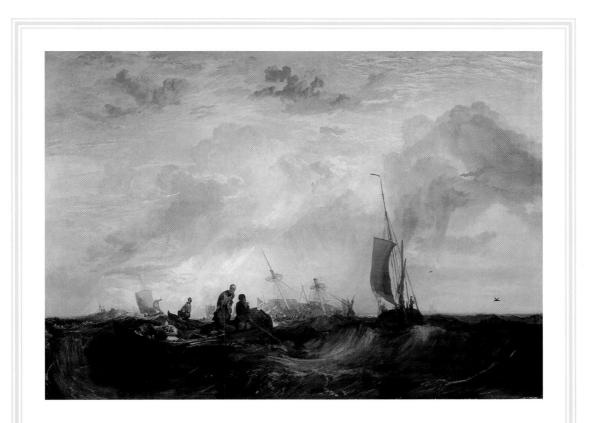

ENTRANCE TO MEUSE,
JOSEPH MALLORD WILLIAM TURNER

Is bliss, then, such abyss
I must not put my foot amiss
For fear I spoil my shoe?
EMILY DICKINSON

s it not our attachment to the shoe that breeds our worry and doubt? The fear of letting go that holds us back from the endless joy of Life itself? Can we truly abandon ourselves to bliss when we are fearful?   A wise man tells the story of a man who fell over the edge of a high cliff and grabbed a tree branch as he fell. He held on to the branch for dear life. Looking down, he saw a dark, bottomless gulf. He yelled for help. God asked if he was calling. "Yes," replied the man. "What do you want?" asked God. "Please, God, please, save me," begged the man. "Let go," God answered.   The fears of loss of control, the unknown and the abyss, deny our souls the very substance for which it hungers and thirsts—life itself in all its wonder and glory, heaven on earth, spiritual joy. Risk is faith. Surrender, and abandon yourself to Life. The constricting shoe of worry and fear will vanish in the blissful celebration of Life as you adventure through its mysteries.   The risk and fear of letting go is best summed up by Henry David Thoreau: "The mass of men lead lives of quiet desperation and go to the grave with the song still in them." Brothers and sisters, move through the fear to faith. Risk. Let go of the old and desperate. Take off the shoe. This well-known saying expresses it so well: "Fear knocked at the door. Faith opened it. And lo, there was no one there!" Joy lies in faith.

YOUNG WOMAN AT THE BEACH, PHILIP WILSON STEER

Happiness is a by-product of an effort to make someone else happy.

GRETA PALMER

Often in our daily lives we reach out to please another, and suddenly we are infused with joy. Recall, rerun, and contemplate one of these acts. Were you blessed with happiness? ▪ A greeter is welcoming people as they enter the room for a meeting. A heavy-burdened, sad man slides in the door. The greeter hesitates at the man's exterior mask of leave-me-alone; in spite of this she musters up a warm, smiling welcome and reaches out her hand. The man looks up, unsure, but then shakes her hand; a sigh of relief, then a smile and grateful eyes break through his mask. The greeter is overjoyed. ▪ How fulfilling for the greeted and the greeter! A simple gesture, yet great effort by the greeter was needed to prevail over the unspoken barriers. When we unconditionally reach out to another to bring him or her happiness, heart-felt joy surges from within. When our efforts are not received, we need to reexamine our own motives. If joy abides, we know we gave the best we could. Otherwise whom were we really trying to please? ▪ Often the effort made on behalf of another is at the expense of ourselves—our time, our energy, our money. But then again, isn't that what giving and effort mean? Perhaps that is the secret to the by-product of the happiness we receive: We are focusing outside ourselves to bring happiness to another. ▪ Make that effort today. Smile and find a compliment for the checkout person in the supermarket. Do it again tomorrow and the next day. Become what you practice. Use Mary Carolyn Davies's *Prayer for Every Day:* "Let me be joy, be hope! Let my life sing!"

DANCE IN THE COUNTRY, PIERRE-AUGUSTE RENOIR

People need joy quite as much as clothing.
Some of them need it far more.

MARGARET COLLIER GRAHAM

Clothing protects our outside; joy protects our inner being. Clothing complements and enhances our bodies; joy complements and enhances our walk in the world. Picture impoverished circumstances: rural poverty or violent inner-city chaos. The teacher, the social worker, the nurse, the priest—all see the physical needs for improved food, shelter, and clothing. The most effective of these sees the need for hope and plants the seeds of joy. The teacher not only teaches but also uses every available tool—field trips, videos, role models—to bring a better world within the grasp of the student. In his book, *In Pursuit of Happiness,* psychologist Dr. Norman M. Bradburn writes "It is the lack of joy in Mudville, rather than the presence of sorrow that makes the difference." No matter our circumstances, we may all continue to wallow in the mud of apathy and/or resignation. In Mudville there is no light at the end of the tunnel, no hope in the future. These people need joy far more than clothing. Many of us give charitably: contributions of money, food, and clothing. Remember also to give the gift of yourself. A kind word of encouragement, a listening ear and heart, sharing how to build the fire, one stick at a time, kindling the spark into the flame of hope. Let joy and hope open up the glory of life in our world to all.

SUNFLOWERS, VINCENT VAN GOGH

Who is the happiest of men? He who values the merits of others.

And in their pleasure takes joy, even as though 'twere his own.

JOHANN WOLFGANG VON GOETHE

Happy indeed is the person who sees the goodness of others. This person is not comparing. Esteem of another's worth leaves no room in one's heart or mind for envy or jealousy. This is easier said than done. ▪ Have you ever felt envy or jealousy for a friend who has deservedly received a promotion, a reward, or even a compliment for work well done? Or felt resentment when someone is asked to take a leadership role in a situation that you think you could handle better? ▪ These are very human feelings; we all have them at times. Recognize them for what they are: love failing. What are these negative qualities telling us about ourselves? Envy, jealousy, resentment—the dark side of love—are reflecting our own inner needs for universal love. Our personalities are trying to meet these needs in a negative way. Love distorted changes virtues to destructive character traits. Fear, loss, and uncertainty underlie envy and jealousy, resulting in pain. At these times our limited understanding conflicts with our soul's unlimited, unconditional purpose to live in unity with the principle of love. Our very human selves have turned away from love. We are separated from the essence of Life, blocked from the love of our brothers and sisters. The spiraling effect of these negative emotions closes the door to happiness. ▪ Child of love, open your heart to the universal flow of love. Let love flood your personality drowning the me, me, me. Be lifted on the living waters to your soul's purpose of unity in love. Love heals and transforms. Love our brothers and sisters; enjoy their achievements and abundance. Joy is one of the many fruits of universal love.

THE YELLOW HAYSTACK, PAUL GAUGUIN

What is the worth of anything
But for the happiness 'twill bring?
RICHARD OWEN CAMBRIDGE

magine a world where we humans took an action or verbalized our emotions and/or thoughts only when and if the outcome would result in happiness for ourselves and others. Anger, resentment, bitterness, jealousy, envy, and greed would no longer pollute our external and internal environments. What a joyful place to be! ▪ Let us begin with ourselves. Here is an example: A male executive asked a female manager struggling to build her career to do the file clerk's task of retrieving past records from the warehouse. He offered her an extra day off as a reward. The woman was irate. She went to the restroom to hide her tears of frustration, anger, and fear. She calmed down and thought it through. Instead of retorting with anger, she returned and said to her boss with a smile, "I would be happy to do this for you, but rather than an extra day off I would like to take the lead on the next project." Her boss, surprised and taken aback, said, "All right." ▪ In this instance, rather than dump her justified anger on her boss and coworkers and create an environment of tension, the woman retreated and allowed herself to experience privately all the hurt and anger. Alone with her thoughts, she came up with a solution that would please both herself and her boss. ▪ Difficult and trying circumstances can bring happiness. Be responsible for your own negative thoughts and emotions. Reflect, count to ten, think. How can I bring some joy to this mess? There is always a way. It is the path of love. We can make our own rooms—our hearts and souls, our places of living and work—sanctuaries of love, light, peace, and joy.

SADNESS OF THE KING, HENRI MATISSE

Whate'er there be of Sorrow/I'll put off till To-morrow,
And when To-morrow comes, why then/'Twill be To-day and Joy again.

Today's sorrow rides on suffering and pain of the past, whether of the past moment, hour, day, week, month, year, or decade. Let today's joy heal the wounds of the past. Do you really want to wallow in sorrow? Will you mindlessly irritate and pick at wounds that eternal Life has healed, is healing, and continues to heal right now? Will you choose to miss your friend's smile, your child's play, your spouse's touch, right now because you are too busy wandering around the empty, lifeless rooms of the past from which others have now moved on? Today find something, anything, that brings joy: a memory, a person, a place, a song, the sky, a raindrop, a sharing, helping another, a bonbon. Experience the joy fully. Be there in it. Cherish it. Bring the feeling of joy, your elated spirit, with you into whatever, whomever the day brings. Transfer it into the moment of whatever you are doing. If there is a task you dislike—doing dishes, vacuuming, commuting, computer spreadsheets—find one thing about that task that brings pleasure—like water running over your hand or gratitude that you have a home to vacuum, a job to commute to, a computer to ease mathematical tasks. Move into the eternal now. Whoosh through the clouds of sorrow. Allow the sun to rise within you. Just for this day let your joy be.

PINKS AND CLEMATIS IN A CRYSTAL VASE,
EDOUARD MANET

He who bends to himself a Joy/Does the winged life destroy;
But he who kisses the Joy as it flies/Lives in Eternity's sunrise.

WILLIAM BLAKE

Follow your joy. It is leading you into the eternal oneness of each moment. Your joy is speaking to and for you; it is saying thank you to the harmony within and without; thank you for teaching me through joy to let go and obey Thy will. ■ Here we are enjoying a game with our children, talking intimately on the phone with a friend, or immersed in reading a book. Happiness, peace, fun, ease—flowing with time and space—abounds. Time control sees the clock, an old thought form tells us it is time to begin supper. We are losing the joy. What to do? One of us abruptly breaks off the moment and grudgingly starts dinner. Another splits the moment, trying to do both, going back and forth to the joyful activity and preparing dinner; confusion erupts. Still another stays with the harmonious will of the current, allowing the joyful activity to continue, knowing it will flow naturally into hunger and dinner preparations. How difficult it is not to manipulate joy! ■ What exactly is required here? Observe the clock's time. Think the dinner thought. But don't let the time and thought control your behavior. Bring your attention back to the moment and let the joy infuse your whole being. Love the joy as eternal time gently guides you to the completion of this moment and activity into the joy of the next. ■ As Chaucer wrote, "Joy of this world, for time will not abide; From day to night it changeth as the tide." Let go and let God carry you along the path of eternity, for it transcends time and space and is the same yesterday, today, and tomorrow.

THE RIVER OF LIFE, WILLIAM BLAKE

I wish you all the joy that you can wish.

SHAKESPEARE

How do you wish? What do you desire? What are your secret longings? What are you affirming, claiming? Will joy spring forth? Consider the woman, head of her household, who provided well for her children and achieved her professional career goals by working days, and juggling evenings and weekends between her children and M.B.A. studies. Her belief and trust in prayer focused on a career to make money. Her work and the consequent money, however, did not bring any joy. Again her spiritual devotions revealed yet another truth. In Jessie Rittenhouse's words,

> *I bargained with life for a penny,*
> *only to learn, dismayed,*
> *That any wage I had asked of life*
> *Life would have paid.*

Indeed, our desires, intent, prayers are answered. Within those anwers are new lessons. Just as this woman did, we too can cast off old man-learned belief systems and become aware of the abundance in the kingdom. This woman listened to joy guiding her back into an old dream of being a painter. She became willing to risk a career change that would bring this joy. She acted on this through prayer, a painting class and a strong belief that this new life would happen in God's time. A decade later it did. Are you limiting yourself, others, possibilities? There is a popular saying, "Be careful what you pray for, you might get it." In Sir Charles Sedley's words, "Tis cruel to prolong a pain and to defer a joy." If you would have joy, remember joy in your wishes.

FOUR TREES, EGON SCHIELE

A happy life must be to a great extent a quiet life,
for it is only in an atmosphere of quiet that true joy can live.

BERTRAND RUSSELL

Can we hear the soft whisper of the loved one amid the clatter and clang of our whirlwind busyness? Have you found your quiet place? ▪ One day a young man summoned his courage and asked his associate, "How can you just do nothing for five minutes so many times during the day? Is something the matter?" The man admired this woman's quiet, focused work habits in their hectic, ruffled office atmosphere. She replied, "I read an article on productivity and meditation. Not only did it advocate contemplation time at home, it also suggested spending five minutes meditating before every hour of a task. It claimed the task would be completed in twice the time it used to take. It works. I become totally involved in the task. I really enjoy my work now." ▪ According to Tibetan doctrine, "Meditation is the clarifier of a beclouded mind." And the Native American has a saying, "Listen or thy tongue will keep thee deaf." Contemplation, or meditation, is simply a method for entering that place where we are alone, stripped of the garments of all the senses, thoughts, and emotions we attach to the turmoil of the material world around us. ▪ When we find the path to that calm, quiet place within us, true joy rises from the fountain of the eternal spring as we are washed of the world's frantic activity. We leave our quiet place renewed and reconciled by the glory of eternal light and the peace that passes all understanding.

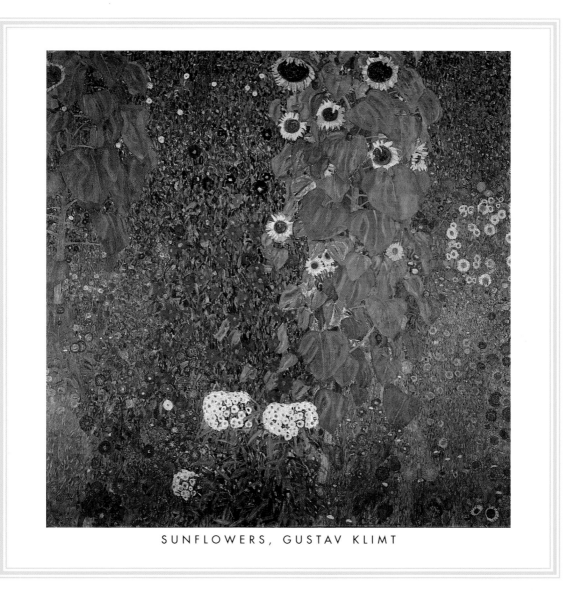

SUNFLOWERS, GUSTAV KLIMT

If we, therefore, would have life in the form of health, happiness and substance, and have it
more abundantly, we must look, move and speak only in the direction of life.

REBECCA BEARD

Every thought, emotion, word, sensation, action, reaction—everything moves either with the constructive power of Life or against it. Current that is reversed short-circuits and destroys.　How swiftly harsh criticism dulls the life force. Have you noticed the lively dog or cat crouch and tremble when harshly punished? Observe the behavior of a child or coworker who is being verbally assualted or condemned. The fight-or-flight instinct triggers an angry retort or angry retreat. Watch how a child or animal moves toward love when the same message is given in a loving way, in a gentle voice with the soul of the eyes contacting the soul of the other.　Life moves forward. Life does not know destruction. As one vessel of life disintegrates, dies, or changes, the life force simply moves through another vessel. Life goes on. Any undisciplined lapse—reactions from our lesser selves—has the same power to destroy. Be used by and use the power of life for the good of all.　It means lifting our consciousness into the awareness of life's perfection. Be subject only to the laws of the spirit. "Be wise as a serpent and as harmless as a dove" (Matthew 10:16). What discipline this takes! We are challenged with our every thought, emotion, word, and deed to act in the direction of life—the healing power that abundantly gives health, meaning, and joy.

MAMMOTH HOT SPRINGS, "YELLOWSTONE,"
THOMAS MORAN

You have to sniff out joy, keep your nose to the joy trail.

BUFFY SAINTE-MARIE

Rather like the cat hunting its prize, there are times to retreat, be still, walk, run, crouch, and jump. Like a maze, some trails are dead ends, others lead us in circles back to the beginning. Yet with each path taken, the faint glimpse of the once-invisible golden thread brightens and leads us through our seeking. ■ What are some of the obstacles and mistaken turns? One is "making a mountain out of a molehill." Pare your life, your trail, down to its real size—this place, this time, these few people, now. Another is to recognize problems you have brought on yourself. Are you sniffing along another's trail uninvited, trying to tell him or her what to do? Allow others to move in their own direction. And what about trying to please everyone? It is futile and exhausting to try to please those who really don't care or can never be pleased. Give from within as the golden thread leads you. And are you still letting other people hurt your feelings? Pay no heed to the trap of criticism; let go of the unnecessary suffering. The golden thread will always support you. ■ Well, you say there are real problems. Agreed. But can we control all circumstances—people and things? The remedies of blaming, anger, getting even, and self-pity only bring misery. The "yellow-brick road" is paved with acceptance and surrender. ■ As the journey of joy progresses, we rely less on ourselves. To the extent that we believe and trust the golden thread, it brightens and expands. It is easier to see and follow. Divine providence unfolds and lights the joy trail.

BEECH TREES, GUSTAV KLIMT

God's ultimate purpose in all suffering is joy.
ELIZABETH ELLIOT

Behind suffering and pain, truth reveals hidden joy. "Seek and ye shall find" the paradoxical lessons of the continual unfolding of love, light, peace, and joy. ■ A successful lawyer, severely handicapped by illness, is unable to continue working. A joyless life-habit of incessant activity, work, and worry comes to a halt. Anger, pain, and self-pity reign. As he reflects on the missed professional life that was, he begins to see how wonderful it was. The ordinary family life of spouse and children that used to irritate now seems so special and touching. Gratitude and joy enrich the work life that had once been cares and woes. ■ Pain is a message to change our attitudes and behavior. Denial and resistance to spiritual truth—to the as-yet-unseen and ever-changing nature of all—causes pain and suffering. Accepting and blessing "what is" dissipates the resistance. We do not need to lose our way in the black hole. We only need to go through it, keeping our mind's eye on the light that heals. Light illuminates that which is hidden in darkness; new insights, lessons and understanding bubble up through the murky whirlpool of our unconsciousness into the clear, sparkling sunlight of consciousness. ■ As light cleanses and heals the ache and scream of pain, the old everyday life is transfigured. The joy is in learning to see with God's eyes. "I found more joy in sorrow than you could find in joy," wrote Sara Teasdale. Light illuminates our reality into a higher truth. Our inner being rejoices. ■ *Divine Creator, most glorious One, for this day, for each moment let me see Your light with Your eyes in every person, every event, every thing.*

THE ANGEL STANDING IN THE SUN,
JOSEPH MALLORD WILLIAM TURNER

How soon a smile of God can change the world!
How we are made for happiness—how work Grows play, adversity a winning fight!
ROBERT BROWNING

imple blessings from the Creator—a kind word or a smile of understanding in a difficult situation, a tree growing up out of concrete on a city street, children romping gleefully in raked piles of autumn leaves, a timely hug from a friend—change the way we see the world. ▪ Two families living next door are outside on a warm, sunny Saturday afternoon working in the yard. In one yard there is singing, laughing, playing. Father and son talk sports. Mother hums as she weeds. The younger ones water themselves and the garden. In the other yard the mother bosses the scowling son and silent father. The younger ones hide. One family sees the work as an opportunity for the family to be together and to enhance the beauty of their home. The other family resents the yard chores; silent anger rumbles. ▪ Just as the earth and the moon have a dark and a light side, so do all people, places, and things. Which do you see? The light or the shadow? Opportunities or drudgery? When we see the blessings, work becomes joyful productivity; hardship becomes victory. ▪ Wilferd A. Peterson sums it up in *The Art of Living*: "Happiness doesn't come from doing what we like to do but from liking what we have to do . . . from putting our hearts in our work and doing it with joy and enthusiasm . . . and from the afterglow of satisfaction that comes after the achievement of a difficult task that demanded our best." ▪ Enjoy the happiness for which we were created.

MARCELLE LENDER DANCING THE BOLERO IN CHILPERIC,
HENRI DE TOULOUSE-LAUTREC

Happiness is a habit—cultivate it.

ELBERT HUBBARD

Happiness and joy flow from those thoughts, attitudes, and actions that bring us into harmony with the universe. We are meant to choose and practice spiritual principles. Belief is not necessary; practice is. ■ This is too difficult, you think. The fact that you are reading this indicates interest. Think back to your last newly acquired activity. It may be roller blading, learning the computer, dancing, gardening, playing the piano. Doesn't your current state of proficiency reflect a desire to learn, a decision of will, thoughts of how, when, where and the practice of doing it? The frequency, the intent, the concentration and the discipline all contribute to this new ability. Is happiness not worth the same attention and time? ■ Do you afflict yourself and others with a chronic habit of unhappiness? Transform this time and energy drain into a nourishing habit of happiness. Throughout each day stop whatever you are doing, be still, and rhythmically breathe in the light. As the separate "me" becomes the universal "us," allow yourself to surrender to the music of the spheres, the creative power of spirit. In this stillness practice watching your thoughts, feelings, and actions and become aware of all negativity. Understand the feelings, but focus on behavior and thoughts. Thoughts and actions determine feelings. If we choose to love and act lovingly toward our parents, children, spouses, and associates, the feeling of love will follow. Open your heart to the love within. Choose love. Be love—lovable and loving. Practice love. Are you happier now? ■ Leo Tolstoy wrote, "I am always with myself, and it is I who am my tormentor." Cultivating a deliberate habit of stillness, harmony, and loving attitudes changes the balance of power each and every time we practice *doing* it. The new habit of happiness becomes a way of being.

LA JOIE DE VIVRE, PABLO PICASSO

Children love and want to be loved and they very much prefer the joy of accomplishment to the triumph of hateful failure. Do not mistake a child for his symptom.

DR. ERIK ERIKSON

A child radiates inner peace and joy when his activity has been recognized as an accomplishment. Rebellion triumphs when it meets criticism. The small boy was laying out the train tracks of his wooden train set with his father. The straight portion was perfect. He hooked the second curve piece reversed. The father quickly grabbed it and said, "No, that is all wrong. The sharp S-curve will derail the train." "No, no," retorted the boy, holding the impossible curve tightly in place. "You told me I could do it. This is the way it goes." Rather than fail, the boy rebelled. How can we reframe this vignette to bring about harmony and joy rather than disharmony and discordant rebellion? What are the father's choices? Praise his son on the perfect straight portion; encourage and support the boy each step of the way; remain silent, quietly loving and caring for the boy, allowing his son to discover and learn for himself? The way of love and joy does not destroy a child's faith in his own abilities. Just as the boy discovers how the train rides smoothly in harmony with the track, the father is able to learn to be in harmony with the learning of his son. The humiliation and shame of being wrong are averted through thoughtful choices. Loving assurance provides the comfort and security that encourage an inner, deep joy of accomplishment. Remember, we are all children learning every moment. Be like a child. Learning is a joyful process.

MOULIN HUET BAY, GUERNSEY, PIERRE-AUGUSTE RENOIR

Sweets with sweets war not, joy delights in joy.

L ike attracts like, as in magnets and electrical poles. The pain of grief diminishes when someone who has been through a similar situation shares their own. We know we aren't alone. Joy likewise is contagious and builds hope. ▪ What is our human reaction when someone lashes out in anger toward us? Whether the anger toward us is justified or unjustified, whether we act out verbally or physically, our immediate reaction is anger. Observe your reaction to love, joy, kindness, grief, impatience, irritabilty. Anger begets anger. Hate begets hate. Love begets love. Kindness begets kindness. Joy begets joy. Light begets light. Life begets life. ▪ Do you get it? Nature's law reflects this axiom in the seen—the physical, material world as well as—the unseen in the emotional, mental, and spiritual levels. For every action there is an equal reaction. ▪ Begin now with yourself to transform the negative patterns in this world. Lay each dark nature, whether yours or another's, on the altar of forgiveness. Rise anew in the light. Reap what you sow!

Lord, make me an instrument of your peace.
Where there is hatred, let me sow love;
Where there is injury, pardon;
Where there is doubt, hope;
Where there is darkness, light;
And where there is sadness, joy.

SAINT FRANCIS

CANTIQUE, MARC CHAGALL

The spider's most attenuated thread
Is cord, is cable, to man's tender tie
On earthly bliss; it breaks at every breeze.
EDWARD YOUNG

Have you noticed how a comment, a scowl, seeing another's pain or anger can infringe on your moments of joy? How fleeting and tenuous our contentment and bliss! ▪ The parents who take their three-month-old baby to the doctor and, beaming with joy, say, "Look, he can hold his head up." The doctor, with characteristic dry humor, replies, "Can't walk yet, can he?" The squelch of joy. Or take a scene unrelated to you: You are walking down the street filled with the joy of blossoming spring; a young man and woman round the corner are shouting at each other, their faces contorted with anger. Horror, pain, sadness, or anger bombard that joy. ▪ We all know people who see only the doom and gloom in situations, and see the worst in people. The positive, the joy, the light is twisted and deflected. Silently pray for them. Imagine them filled and surrounded with light. Bring the light back in and around yourself. Does your earthly bliss return? ▪ Just as the spider has many threads in its protective and nourishing web, we have a similar web of light protecting and nourishing us. How quickly the spider retreats, adjusts, and mends; likewise we are able to be renewed in joy. Just bring the mind back to light. ▪ As William James wrote in *The Varieties of Religious Experience*, "How to gain, how to keep, how to recover happiness is in fact for most men at all times the secret motive of all they do, and of all they are willing to endure."

IMPRESSION, SUNRISE, CLAUDE MONET

We have no more right to consume happiness
without producing it than to consume wealth without producing it.
GEORGE BERNARD SHAW

am responsible, therefore I should be happy. Duty is to assume responsibility, to be of service, to be entrusted. Look at life, the universe. Are you not in awe? Are we not stewards of all this glory? ▪ Two young men walked side by side. One kept his eyes turned downward, studying the cracks in the sidewalk. The other looked up, smiling at teeming life—passersby, our awesome inventiveness of skyscrapers, our multifarious products displayed in windows, trees growing out of the concrete. Life smiled back at him. People saw this radiant man looking up and smiling. They wondered what it was he saw; they wanted what he had. So they, too, looked up. Whatever, whomever, was on their hearts and minds left at the moment, and they, too, looked up and saw. His happiness touched the joy of life within some of them. The other young man continued to frown at the broken cracks, endlessly going nowhere; he missed it all. ▪ Are you holding onto happiness? Allow your joy to flow through you to others. Let it be seen. Celebrate life openly. Joy empowers both giver and receiver. Learn from the words of the Mundaka Upanishad, "From joy springs all creation. By it is sustained, toward joy it proceeds, and to joy it returns."

A BOUQUET OF FLOWERS, PIERRE-AUGUSTE RENOIR

Capacity for joy Admits temptation.

ELIZABETH BARRETT BROWNING

Wise is the person who understands that momentary pleasures can lead to remorse, regret, trouble and pain. Plato suggests that joy and pleasure are "the bait of sin"—temptation. ▪ Have you ever tipped the balance of the joy scales? Have you ever been the joyless receiver of another's pleasure? Haven't we all! The-one-drink-too-many changes a jovial gathering to one of embarrassment or chaos; gluttonous portions of food take satiety and contentment to stupefaction; indiscriminant and thoughtless sex has troubled the world since the beginning; entertaining talk becomes puffed-up ego or hurtful sarcasm. Jolly folly, joy is not. ▪ Has giving in to the temptations of excitement and pleasure enslaved you to destructive, obsessive habits? Wake up. Learn to discern. Think through the consequences of your actions. Remember the hangover of acted-out temptations. Discomfort, pain, lack of inner joy just may be a *no* or *stop* signal for our excesses. Let wisdom and inner joy replace the fleeting pleasure disguised as joy. ▪ How wide or narrow is the eye of your needle? To continue to experience real, deep, true joy the eye of the needle narrows as we live and learn life's lessons. The delicate balance enters our awareness. ▪ As Epicurus wrote, "When we say, then, that pleasure is the end and aim of life, we do not mean the pleasures of the prodigal or the pleasures of sensuality. . . . By pleasure we mean the absence of pain in the body and of trouble in the soul."

LOVERS UNDER A RED TREE, MARC CHAGALL

ajor losses and disappointments capture the heart in sorrow. Joy ricochets off the stone walls we build to ward off any further hurt. Deep within the hardening heart, imprisoned joy waits to unite with the joy of all. ■ The death of a parent, a spouse, or a child is an enormous loss. The tragedy alters our lives beyond anything we can imagine. Anguish lodges in the rooms of our soul. The tears solidify. ■ "Why?" our tested human spirit asks through intellect and reason, "Why am I so alone and tormented even among my loving friends? God, why have you abandoned me?" Crisis announces the hour in our belief when we go it alone. Summon all your courage and strength. Daybreak awaits us on the peak as illumination awakens us to awe. ■ Continue to climb the mountain of seeking, one foot in front of the other. You will reach the top. Be that person who accepts what is. Through acceptance comes the gift of visionary understanding. In that lonely, intuitive leap of faith truth frees us. Light crumbles the stone walls around our hearts. Joy is released. Our hearts are no longer separated from the oneness that is all.

THE GRAND CAYON OF THE YELLOWSTONE,
THOMAS MORAN

Joy is the most effective and far reaching stimulant known to man.
Grief weakens every function and organ while joy strengthens them.

DR. ROBERT ASSAGIOLI

ur whole being—every cell, every atom, and the voids inbetween—hums and sings with the vitality that joy brings. Sadness brings heaviness and tiredness that weakens. ■ Two men lay motionless recovering from major operations. Death hovered. Both men had family and friends visiting, cards and flowers. Yet the environment of each man's limited space was different. One had colorful pictures painted by his grandchildren and cards tacked on the wall, bright flowers were within sight; joyful music played; family and friends spoke only words of encouragment, love, and humor. His space vibrated with life. The other man's area was heavy with fear and worry. Cards and flowers were neatly tucked out of the way. Whispering among family about a changed future persisted. The patient surrounded with the joy of life left the hospital earlier than expected. The other man went into a nursing home. ■ Fear drains and robs us of our essential life force. Negative states inhibit brain messages to our body, create tension, and restrict the flow of energy. This dynamic life force powers our minds, emotions, and will. The more we let the inexhaustible power of life flow freely through us, the more we receive. We call it healing, our bodies responding to the wholeness of Life itself. ■ In *The Doctor's Job*, Dr. Carl Binger spoke of "splinters in the soul," "More people are sick because they are unhappy than there are those who are unhappy because they are sick." Turning away from life weakens. Rejoicing in life strengthens, both ourselves and those around us.

VASE WITH NASTURTIUMS AND "THE DANCE,"
HENRI MATISSE

Oh, frabjous day! Callooh! Callay!
He chortled in his joy.

LEWIS CARROLL

L ive this day with the joy of just being a part of all the glory of creation. Whether you are alone or sharing with another, feel the beauty of the world as it pulses with unseen life and love. ▪ What about the grandfather who, observing his grandson's distress as his parents orchestrate his day with their well-intentioned, achievement and character-building activities, says, "Let's go fishing now"? The mother and father look at each other speechless, both knowing grandfather has never fished in the many years they've known him. The boy's father hushes his wife's objections as their beaming son and the whistling grandfather disappear, hand-in-hand, across the lawn toward the wood and very distant pond. ▪ How often we miss the little miracle of the moment: a mother's heart enveloping her baby with love on a subway; a butterfly in the act of becoming as it shakes its wings free from the cocoon. Our *ought-tos*, *have-to*s, and *shoulds* chain us to the habits and beliefs of the past; these thoughts and feelings control our controlling even as our mental busyness and planning prevent us from seeing with the universal eye of now. Right now, stop: Listen, See, Smell, Feel. Haven't the thoughts vanished? You are being made new in that moment of still awareness. Through this process joy begins. ▪ Grandfather and grandson fished for hours, in total contentment and in harmony with all of divine creation. And how they chortled with joy on their return. ▪ As Thoreau wrote, "Many men go fishing their entire lives without knowing it is not fish they are after."

BATTLE SCENE FROM THE COMIC OPERA
"THE SEAFARER," PAUL KLEE

A sorrow that's shared is but half a trouble,
But a joy that's shared is a joy made double.

JOHN RAY

When we tell another person about a bothersome problem, the burden we have held in our hearts is lightened. A joy retold is relived by ourslevves and brings joy and hope to another. ▪ The young manager hadn't planned to share a secret that caused him remorse, regret, guilt, and fear that he might repeat his mistake, but an older colleague shared a similar experience he had had years earlier. He went on to express gratitude for the insights he had gained by confronting the issue and sharing it. He rejoiced in the inner journey that had transformed him and changed his behavior. The younger man, wide-eyed, blurted out his unintentional transgression of his marriage vows. As the small group of men listened and shared and talked of similar situations, temptations, lessons learned and changed behavior, the young manager realized he was not alone. His remorse, regret, and guilt were beginning to break up. He felt great relief. Hope began to replace fear. ▪ Simple sharing brought a secret burden out of the darkness of the soul into the light of truth. The young man was human after all, a flawed human in a flawed world. We are not divinely perfect, are we? Joy, always the victor, swallows sorrow. ▪ Sharing sorrow lifts the yoke. Sharing joy releases joy. Witnessing plants the seeds of encouragement, humility, and hope. In Byron's words, "All who joy would win, must share it,—Happiness was born a twin."

THE SWALLOWS, EDOUARD MANET

God is the primary source of joy and hope for man.

HIS HOLINESS JOHN PAUL II

Seek God, the source, and in finding the kingdom within, you will find ever-lasting joy. "Thy kingdom come, thy will be done, on earth as it is in heaven." ▪ The woman seeing her friend's peace and inner joy, asked, "Where does your joy come from? Your life has been so difficult, yet you seem truly happy." The friend said, "It was a long journey and often a struggle. Ever since I was a teenager and began to question the existence of God, I have been seeking answers. Over the years I studied and/or practiced most of the major, some minor, religious and philosophical systems, including various Christian denominations. Although I was learning and moving along a spiritual path, an inner longing remained. I always seemed to be reaching outside of myself for God. There came a day when friends, who had a faith I admired, suggested I invite the Lord into my heart. Despite my intellectual doubts, I decided I had nothing to lose. So I did as they suggested. ▪ "My life turned around a hundred and eighty degrees and has not been the same since. It was the point of transformation—the end of seeking, the beginning of new life. It is simple. God, creator of all, can do anything, and He can manifest Himself in human form. In all my studies and practices it is knowing the Lord personally—talking to Him daily about every little thing, listening to His guidance and occasional chiding, thanking Him for everything including the hard lessons—that has brought joy and hope beyond all expectation." ▪ As the Pope says, the "good news" is an invitation to joy.

ROUEN CATHEDRAL, HARMONY IN BLUE AND GOLD,
FULL SUNSHINE, CLAUDE MONET

PERMISSIONS AND ACKNOWLEDGEMENTS

Grateful acknowledgement is made to Art Resource and Scala/Art Resource, National Museum of American Art/Art Resource, Giraudon/Art Resource, Erich Lessing/Art Resource, Bridgeman/Art Resource, National Collection of American Art/Art Resource, Tate Gallery, London/Art Resource, and Superstock for permission to use the works of art printed herein.

Grateful acknowledgement is made to Ayer Company Publishers, Inc., Manchester, New Hampshire 03102, for permission to reprint "My Wage" and "Debt" by Jesse Rittenhouse. All rights for the world administered by Ayer Company Publishers, Inc.

Grateful acknowledgement is made to Artists' Rights Society for permission to use ENTRANCE TO MEUSE and THE ANGEL STANDING IN THE SUN by Joseph Mallord William Turner, © ARS, Tate Gallery, London, Great Britain, and to use THE GRAND CANYON OF THE YELLOWSTONE, RAINBOW OVER THE GRAND CANYON OF THE YELLOWSTONE, and MAMMOTH HOT SPRINGS, YELLOWSTONE by Thomas Moran, © ARS, National Museum of American Art, Washington D.C., U.S.A.